COLLAGE

Distributors in U. K.

FOUNTAIN PRESS LTD.

45 The Broadway, Tolworth, Surrey KT6 7DW.
Tel: 01-3907768 (3 lines)

COLLAGE

FERIT ISCAN

 Parramón

Published by Parramón Ediciones, S.A.
Lepanto, 264-4.º 08013-Barcelona (Spain)

© José M.ª Parramón Vilasaló
First impression, March 1986

Register Book Number: 785
Legal Deposit: B. 14.628-86
ISBN: 0 86343 013 9

Printed in Spain by SIRVEN GRAFIC, S.A.
Gran Vía, 754-08013-Barcelona

Distributed in the United Kingdom by
FOUNTAIN PRESS LTD.
45, The Broadway, Tolworth,
Surrey KT6 7DW

All correspondence concerning the content of this volume should be addressed to
Parramón Ediciones, S.A.

Contents

«At heart, I could not really understand why, in the same way that we used paints to create a picture, it is not possible to use materials such as old train tickets, pieces of wood, cloakroom tickets, pieces of string, bicycle spokes, and so on... in a word, all that old bricabrac stored away in an attic or among piles of rubbish. Somehow I thought that working with those materials would be like giving my style a certain social viewpoint and I soon discovered that this activity was a real personal pleasure for me. As time passed, this was the main reason for continuing with that kind of composition. I named this new technique based on the use of such materials Merz*».

Kurt Schwitters (1887-1948)
Hannover, 1928
(From the «Book on mixed techniques», Férit Iscan-Bordas Ed.)

---

* *Kurt Schwitters, poet and abstract painter was the inventor of Merz. The word «Merz» appeared in each one of his collages. The origin was the name of a bank (Commerz und Privatbanc).*

preface

I have been a painter for thirty years and I have always been motivated by the wish to know every new artistic manifestation in the field of creativity.

Some reject new tendencies automatically, but for me, I believe the only thing that matters is the need to create and the result obtained. I leave it to the critics to say whether «this» is better than «that» and vice versa.

It is quite obvious that making a collage, with its conforming elements clearly displayed, requires techniques that are very different from those used in the so-called «traditional» painting, a concept, in fact, hardly containing a specific meaning any longer.

The materials change continuosly in a collage, so an adequate technique is needed for each work. Everything has to be invented once and again in the field of collage. After some time, though, some concepts picked up here and there seemed to me solid enough to be the basis and starting point for a study of the collage technique. What I have wanted to do in this book is, then, develop the results of my research in this matter. At this point I have to thank the valuable collaboration given by Gilbert Pélissier.

Logically, these pages are included in the frame of artistic activities but they are by no means an intent to compile a complete catalogue of collage and the artists who have practised it up to now. There are so many and their achievements so remarkable!

The examples chosen to illustrate this book seemed to me particularly good, as much for their quality as for their value as a guide to follow.

As far as I'm concerned in my experience as a painter, I can say that practising those techniques, I came to see the relevant place of collage in the creative processes. Some collages derive from painting; others find in painting their perfect complement, and others still have an autonomous expressiveness. Whatever the case, they all take an active part in the expansion of the more recent history of modern art.

Let's then contribute to that expansion. It is my most sincere wish.

FERIT ISCAN

introduction

Art has breathed a new air of freedom since the last century, when the artists from the newer generations started revitalizing the techniques hallowed by time. These artists have opened broader paths to creativeness through their boldness, thus allowing new forms of expression —such as collages, for example— and in a wider sense, all those artistic creations far from traditional painting. In art exhibits nowadays, catalogues usually refer to these manifestations as «collages». In France, the collages produced with the help of solid materials are known as «ensembles» and those with paint in relief are described as «of mixed technique».

These procedures, hardly used before, are becoming more and more usual, but they are still quite unknown to the amateur artist.

The air of freedom mentioned at the beginning has fostered, during the last century, the continuous development and progressive acceptance of expressive media such as collage. Freedom is then in the form as well as in the procedure.

As a summary, then, it is quite clear that even brushes and paint are not indispensable to the creation of a picture.

The use of the general term «collage» is open to any variation the artist's inspiration may produce. For the sake of simplification I have limited the presentation to the three techniques most frequently used nowadays: collages with paper and cardboard, collages with solid materials and collages with paint in relief.

When the artist can work freely, without restriction, fantasy, imagination and curiosity can be fully expressed. In the field of collage, a classic skill in drawing and painting may be an advantage, but there is no doubt that some previous studies of composition are always desirable to learn how to distribute the elements that make up any collage.

Basically, a collage results from the manipulation of paper that has been cut and pasted together, and the result is a plane surface with hardly visible reliefs. The raw material used are old newspapers, magazines, wrapping paper, old pictures, and so on. First of all, the artist looks for the contrast between colours, between textures and colours in paper to achieve bold combinations. These, in turn, will later become harmonious or even unexpected combinations until the work is finished in successive stages.

The cubist painters used this technique on numerous occasions (Braque and Picasso, for example). Without the rigidity of these artists, though, it is possible to work with collages in a much freer way and as a mere diversion. Matisse created some collages from his particular point of view and with unmatched mastery (we will see the illustrations of his work later). As is obvious, the collage with solid materials has a different preparatory basis. The principal elements are solid and consequently give the collage a certain weight and relief. Wood is generally used, whether splintered, charred or painted and grouped to form various shapes. Other elements are objects from current use, such as dolls' heads, old toys, etc. In order to assemble such heterogeneous elements, we will have to use techniques that differ from that used for the collages made with paper: nails, screws, glue for wood, and so on... This type of collage requires greater skills and more careful elaboration. As an example, let's mention the old wooden cases where the printing shops used to keep their type. These cases are a very practical starting point for our first steps in collages with solid materials and may produce surprising effects.

And then, lastly, we have the collage with different reliefs. It is, no doubt, the nearest to painting, since it uses paint as its main element. To create a relief means to combine and

introduction

superimpose a number of paint coatings. The paint, in turn, has additional elements such as sand, sawdust, marble dust, ground pigments and fabrics in different textures. All these elements can be bound with resins and varnishes.

We can apply this technique to a normal painting canvas but wooden or plywood boards are preferable, since these do not suffer from the typical distortions caused by humidity, which can alter the quality of the finished work. In this type of collage, the artist's work is much more decisive, since the preparation and application of the different layers require a definite artistic sense when creating the form.

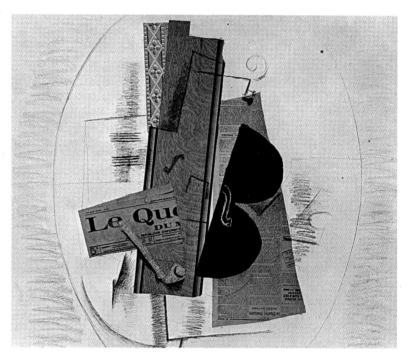

Le Quotidien (or the Daily newspaper); Georges Braque. Pasted paper (74×106). Musée National d'Art Moderne, Paris.

I. HISTORY

1. the followed path

Painting has always expressed the turmoil of its time, through the centuries, through religious, mythological, or lay inspiration, the professional, the amateur, the patronage, its need to create or fulfil aesthetic ambitions. It also expresses the painter's personal motivations, his search for himself, his way toward aestheticism, or in a word, his «style».

Traditional painting was a skill that could be acquired from a master who transmitted his craftmanship to his students in a practical way. They participated in the basic process of the picture or in its final touches, and they also prepared the supports for the painting (boards, canvases, etc.) The classical painter developed his art through a chosen subject, following the examples of his distinguished predecessors. After some time spent learning in the workshop, he travelled through Europe to acquire culture. His first aim was not to do something new but rather «imitate to learn». He did not try to impose his personality since that would happen later, with a reputation based on his work.

In our time, we have grown used to judging different painting styles rather than the degree of vocation shown by the artist. To this end, nothing better than to find out the differences between painters of the same school. It is at least a good approach to painting, an adequate exercise to measure depth, strength or grace. These are troublesome con-

Die Brücke; Rembrandt, 1645. Rembrandt shocked his contempories with some of his paintings.

cepts to analyze, as are all opinions about art. When we look at a picture, we relive part of the painter's existence. History never becomes so tangible as through painting. A picture can be appraised in just a glance, it can be valued instantly and even so, not necessarily ambiguously.

André Malraux says that the beginning of modern painting coincides with Goya's intrusion into the world of art. With Goya, the «expression» —not yet «expressionism»— can be distinguished within the picture and becomes evident to the observer's eyes. For the painter, the expression is a means to confirm an attitude or to make a protest. But little by little the painter, who is an idealist by nature, brings forth

his artistic principles and gets away from any foreign influence. In this sense, the fact of including pieces of the real world into a picture does not necessarily lead to realism.

This difference is clearly revealed in the work of the condemned painters of the end of last century (Van Gogh, Gauguin). The more they were denied their artistic classification, the truer creators they were. The truth is that while giving painting another destiny, they also changed the image of the painter as a character deeply involved in the social scheme.

13

the followed path

In the old Chinese Imperial Court the painter could become counsellor or minister, thus indicating to what extent his wisdom and knowledge of human nature was considered. In Europe, the painter was a subject of kings' protection —or a victim of their demands—. Later, he suffered the consequences of the taking over of power by the people and his work became professional after the extinction of patronage. The paintings he was asked to do were minor works but the artist could let his inspirations flow freely in front of a more democratic but scarcer clientele.

This made him reduce his regular fees or become —he and his profession— bankrupt. The technological revolution that followed, defined the field of work of the painting artist, forcing him to relegate some qualities inherent in his work, such as the observation and search for hidden aspects in a subject. This evolution, announced and denounced in the German Romanticism (E.T. Hoffman was one of the first to talk about it) gradually cornered the painter until his figure became an integral part of the stormy and changing cycle of the time. While wars devasted the world, technological inventions became increasingly important and the human being headed toward our present reality, a specific branch of Art stood out above the others to give a detailed and immediate report of all those events. It was painting, an art without a privileged place in society as before, but

a clear witness of history; an art that needed a change in style and language; an art that did not hesitate to use its weapons —brushes and colours— to protest for having been deferred.

This spark of rebellion was the origin of collages, first practised just before World War I. It was a symptomatic and even logical fact. Mankind was entering a period of extreme confusion and the paths that led to painting opened up for a newcomer that represented both a rupture and a call to attention at the same time: the collage.

The shootings of the 3rd of May; Goya. Malraux once said that modern painting practically started with this Spanish painter.

(Above, right): 14th July in Paris; Van Gogh. A long and painful quest at last enabled Van Gogh to give free rein to this genius.

Apples and oranges; Cézanne. Impressionism meant breaking with what was established and accepted. This rebellious outcry was later seconded by the collage artists.

2. the appearance of collage

In the beginning, collage was only a novel technique, hardly known and seldom used. It did not possess a definite and individual entity, it was just a few stamps stuck here and there... In Japan, however, there is a tradition in collage starting in the 12th century. That collage was hardly known was demonstrated when the cubists «invented» it in the 20th century, while Japanese artists had practised it for a long time.

Apart from the oriental collages, the first references to this art are in Bernard Palissy's ceramics and in the human faces made up of fruits and vegetables by the Milano artist Arcimboldo in the 16th century («The four seasons», Louvre Museum). Even so, the juxtaposition of successive layers on canvas or wood is not peculiar to collage. As a direct predecessor of glued paper —and particularly of some of Matisse's works— let's remember the silhouettes by Lavater. We can appreciate how a gesture is worth more than a thousand words in them (and Lavater lived long before the cinema appeared). The still-lifes by Cézanne opened up the way for «object-painting». His apples were more simple pictorial elements of the picture than imaginative objects offered to the appetite of the observer. The cubists gave the objects an inner life, the pictorial elements came before the subject itself, and in this struggle between fiction (the picture) and reality (the subject), painting was often the winner.

The plastic use of stencilled(*) typographic letters, or of dissembling elements such as the nail that appears at the top of «Jar and violin» (1910) by Braque, already indicate the wish of the artists to bring the matter nearer, to make the ambiguity of the picture stand out by giving it a more concrete personality, halfway between the physical presence of the subject and its image represented on the canvas. The time for dreams was over, and

Fruit bowl and cards; Georges Braque, 1913. Oil, pencil and charcoal on canvas. Musée National d'Art Moderne, Paris.

(*) Stencil: printing drawing; made by applying an inked brush over a metallic plate where elements have been previously cut out.

the «Futuristic Manifesto» denied the old noble materials and promoted the use of unusual elements in painting. It was the way to link with the future. In 1911 Boccioni put together an old window shutter and a head made of plaster of Paris in his «Fusion of a head and a window».

But it was Picasso who set the model of collage to follow in 1912. His «Still life with latticed chair» includes a piece of waxed cloth that imitates the latticed wicker seat of a chair. The systematic use of glued papers could be attributed to Braque, by the end of the analytical period of cubism (1912). It is then that Branque buys in Avignon some wallpapers that imitate wood and marble, and sticks them in areas of the picture that should have been painted. Picasso shared his aesthetic discoveries with Braque in the fertile period 1912-1914, but he preferred newsprint. Perhaps he felt he could express himself better with this material, but maybe he was also unconsciously following the eternal concept of stopping time. A newspaper is, as a matter of fact, an immediate witness of historical happenings.

Portrait of Roland, Mrs. Roland and their daughter Eudora; Lavater, Musée Carnavalet, Paris.
Lavater (1741-1801), a Zurich priest, was a contemplative and mystical man, very famous in his time. He was an active member of several artistic societies and maintained regular correspondance with notable people of the times, such as Goethe, Mme. de Staël, some of Dr. Cagliostro's followers, Swedenborg, although he also had a good rapport with the simplest people. He was a student of physiognomy (the study of the temperament of man through his build, his attitudes and facial features) and this illustration is evident proof of his studies. Notice the gestures suspended in time of each of the characters. They seem to be about to tell us a story. For this reason, Lavater can be considered as anticipating the following collages with pasted paper.

3. glued papers and collages

Whether superimposed on a drawing glued over a canvas, paper is the element more commonly used in the first collages, hence the general name «pasted papers».Besides wallpaper and newspaper, artists often used wrapping or Kraft paper. Kraft paper is used torn or carefully cut, because its even surface recalls the brush strokes in an oil painting, or because of its neutral tone. This tone is equally suitable for charcoal or for lead pencil, and a touch of sepia brings it forward. Wrapping paper served as a palette for many painters; we can see it in «The minotaur» by Picasso at the Museum of Modern Art in Paris.

Once the newspaper is chosen, we study the headlines, how the text lines and the illustrations are arranged, always looking for the right orientation according to our plans. We consider the white of the paper (soon to become yellowish), the black, the angles in the pictures... («Metamorphosis», by Joan Miró).

As it is logical, all kinds of papers were used in the technique of creation of the first collages: music scores, corrugated paper, cinema or theatre programmes, labels, tickets, cardboard or even silk paper and glass paper (the latter recently used by Arroyo for his hatted characters). Each of these elements was —and still is— used by the artists because of its particular nature or colour, its glossy or matt quality, the grain in its texture or other roughness, etc. As a general rule, the definite com-

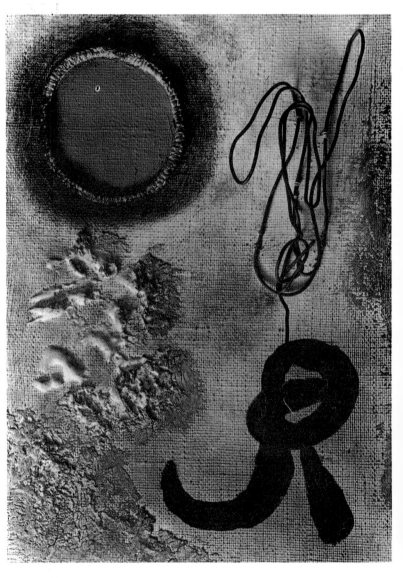

Canvas-object-painting; Miró, Galerie Maeght, Paris. The title defines the three aspects and dimensions that form it. The simple fabric used as the backing has been palely coloured and it looks like an ordinary canvas for a painting. Here the canvas itself, without any paint, is a painting. The object part is given by the plastic-covered wire sewn to the canvas, more or less balanced by the raised shapes at the left. Besides the backing, the painted area is just an oriental character with one stroke, diagonally-opposed to the circle at the top, created with sewn material and paint.

An excellent example of baroque collage.

position is set by the first stroke or tint placed on the canvas. Picasso recreated a wall in a house by means of the wallpaper that would have normally decorated such a house.

Curiously enough, paper, cardboard and other elements acquire a different, personal and poetic dimension while blending into the whole. They lose their individuality little by little, harmonizing the group, eventually giving a distinct seal to the resulting collage. But the history of collage would not end with paper as its only element. Artists started using the most varied elements —most «absurd», some said— such as fabrics, cards, wood, boxes, toys, scrap iron, leather, lamps... Just about anything, as we can see.

In 1912, Juan Gris used a piece of mirror for his work «The bathroom». It was a challenge for the public to face art through something familiar removed from an everyday environment to the painter's canvas. Juan Gris had the audience watch their own reflection in the mirror and thus question the painting done by the cubists by means of his picture, that was half a painting, half an object, half serious, half a joke.

In 1915 Picasso inserted wood between thin gold and silver sheets, and later used feathers, maccaroni, combs, sardine tins... Marcoussis used catalogue covers and pennants for his compositions. The sculptor Laurens used corrugated paper.

The collage also appeared in

other fields, such as the photomontages by Rodchenko, the German, Raoul Hausman, Man Ray; the divertimentos by Duchamp and Charcoune; the canvas-object-painting used by Miró.

Dadaism first, and surrealism later, monopolized the collage technique. Their followers considered it apt to destroy the concept of the classical painting, a concept even the daring cubists had always respected.

Max Ernst did not intend to destroy painting when he created his first collages in Cologne in 1919, before his trip to France. He used illustrations from a natural science catalogue for them. He completed his famous books with the 1900 engraving series «The week of kindness» and «Woman without head».

Abstract art also used collage profusely while also trying to create something eminently plastic out of it, as the cubists did. In 1913, Sonia Delaunay illustrated «Transiberian

View over the bay; Juan Gris, 1921, Private collection.
This is curious example of inverted values, a collage that serves as a subject for the painter. The paintings by Juan Gris are in a very analytical cubist style deriving from the observation by the artist of the plastic impression created by the collage.

Portrait of the artist; Raoul Hausmann, 1923, collage on paper (39,5×26,8), Musée National d'Art Moderne, Paris.

glued papers and collages

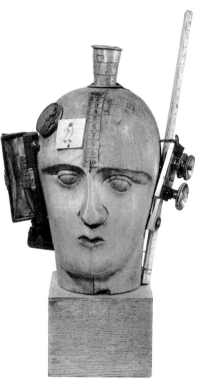

Prose», by Blaise Cendrars, with pasted pieces of paper.
In 1932, Arp tore up his drawings and engravings and then proceeded to make original combinations with the pieces. Magnelli also has works where pasted paper carries his distinctive seal, such as tar paper, glass paper, blotting paper, carbon paper and notebook covers. It can be seen that all collage techniques were «discovered» between 1912 and 1939. The development of these techniques was necessarily halted during World War II. Nazis perse-cuted this art because they considered it degenerate. Collage artists either hid or exiled themselves. Long before the arrival of fascism, however, collage had had time to spread all over Europe, Russia included. The bases for the subsequent pictorial techniques were thus established.

4. collages in the world

Let's refer first of all to the artist who made collage and the manipulation of the most unusual materials the main subject of his work: the German Kurt Schwitters (1887-1948).

He was born in Hannover and studied drawing at the Dresden Academy first and later in Berlin. At the beginning, his work was figurative, but suffered the influence of many of the vanguardists of the early 20th century. He then became involved in the Dadá movement for some time. Schwitters, however, did not want to destroy art (would any real artist want to?); he sought his peculiar artistic horizon starting in 1918, when he turned his back on traditional painting, even the most advanced. He rejected the logical dictatorship of oil and never, or hardly ever again, did he use oil colour except to differentiate fragments of objects incorporated in his work.

This was just the first step. Little by little, materials played a leading role in his abstract compositions, to the point of forming reliefs. He was the first artist to base his aesthetic concepts on elements collected in the rubbish junkyards and similar places. He named his compositions «Merz» which undoubtedly influenced the American painter Rauschenberg a few years later. Schwitter's pasted papers convey a great delicacy in composition and his choice of tones indicate to what extent he worried about the aesthetic aspect of his work at the time. After 1920, the painter widened his «Merz» concept of total art and extended it to

Merzbild 25 A, picture with cloth; Kurt Schwitters, 1920.
Photo library A.S.A.C.
Collage with different materials: papers, rope, wire netting, wood... The elements are divided by paint. Schwitters was the first artist to base his aesthetics on discarded materials. It seems that, after the Great War, he wanted to underline the apparent importance of the useless. «I prefer the absurd —he said— though I recognize this is a purely personal feeling.» His collages later became much more serene and with greater plasticity (he added train tickets, theatre tickets, labels, lace, and so on).

collages in the world

Merzbild 94 - Gründfleck; Kurt Schwitter, Neuenschwander collection, Zurich© Giraudon.

The white ball; Jean Pougny, 1915. Wood and coloured glass (34×50,5×11). Musée National d'Art Moderne, Paris.

theatre, architecture and poetry. At his house in Hannover he engaged in building a huge structure in plaster of Paris and other materials (he would name it «the Schwitters Column»). The column underwent several transformations until it soon invaded all floors and rooms of the house. Unfortunately, it was destroyed by the bombs of World War II. His essays on phonetic poetry qualify Schwitters as a forerunner of «lettristic*» in the field of sound, as the Italian Carra was in the field of plastic

moulding because of his «Prohibited March» (1915), a true explosion of pasted letters.
We have just mentioned an Italian artist and we should add that Italy was not far behind in the art of collage. As a matter of fact, in «Figaro» dated 20th February 1909, the poet Marinetti published a manifesto containing 11 points to induce the poets of the time to pay homage to the industrial civilization with their most typical creations. The message, issued from Paris, was heard in Italy and some painters adapt-

ed their principles to collage, as was the case with Sironi. Another artist, Severini, did a portrait of Marinetti and used a real moustache as a final touch to the mouth.
In 1912 Boccioni (an artist who was missing on the front in World War I in 1916) proposed in his «Manifesto for the futur-

_____

(*) *Typographic: Comparative study of the form of the letters from the artistic aspect.*

istic sculpture» the use of any modern material: wood, cement, iron, horsehair, and so on. The idea was to turn away voluntarily from an academic tradition dating back to the Renaissance. Prampolini was one of the distinguished students of this aesthetic revolution, and he composed his relief-pictures using lace, plaited straw, feathers, sponges, cork and metallic paper.

As we have already seen, the collage exhibitions held by German cubists after 1913 within the group «Der Sturm» influenced Schwitters and Max Ernst decisively. The same phenomenon ocurred in Moscow also in 1913, and two years later in St. Petersburg, where an astonished audience could finally discover the techniques and style used by the French and German vanguard. Malevitch («Lady of the column», 1914) and Tatline adopted these ideas for their reliefs and countereliefs, and Pougny was one of the Russian artists that used collage most effectively. Collages soon established the bases for the subsequent «constructivism», born in Russia to determine the range and expansion of pictures made with pasted paper. In New York, Josep Cornell used boxes, books with drawings, old pictures and so on, applying the collage technique to the cinema. With different clippings, old broken films mounted again differently and other elements he built enigmatic visions. Rose Hobart, New York, Barcelona, Paris, all belong to him.

But all this eruption of ideas and experiences was interrupted by fascism, first in Germany and later also in Italy.

Owl; Joseph Cornell, 1945-46. Collage of different materials in a wooden box. (63×36×16). Musée National d'Art Moderne, Paris.

5. postwar years

In 1947 Henri Matisse presented collage with a new vision, especially due to his book «Jazz». This painter's temperament tended to quietness, luxury and voluptuousness; he did not share the ascetic ideas of cubism that Picasso practised, even when they were very close. Matisse's intention was to give the spectator a feeling of calmness and inner peace. His style was suitable for the use of pasted paper. He redeemed the function of paper as the basic support and ennobled it until he obtained the refined shape of a human figure, mainly female. Matisse played with different colours of paper —he used blue for his monochromatic work,— cutting out the shapes directly with the scissors and obtaining a subtle outline such as would be possible with a pencil. He then proceeded to paste these shapes over a neutral, white or unbleached backing.

Matisse's evolution towards collage differed greatly from that of other artists. His compositions are valid for flat figures over a background and the explanation lies in the fact that being quite old his sight was very weak.

His work does not present dissonant tones nevertheless. What he was after, time and again, was the materialization

Jazz; Henri Matisse, 1947. Pasted paper (42×32,6) Kupferstichkabinet SMPK, Berlin.
In 1946, after a period of eclipse (during and after World War II), Matisse used his personal technique again in his book «Jazz». Old and sick, he forgot his brushes because «scissors can show even more sensibility than a pencil», as he said. He cut out his figures from coloured paper, in this case blue, and later pasted them over a uniform background. The critic Frank Elgar described this collage as «the modern equivalent of the typical medieval illumination».

of a poetic and idealistic moment suspended in time, of a reflection of reality. For that, he used paper cuttings, since they are as efficient as free brush stroke and departed from the techniques used by the cubists and their followers. Matisse's plasticity was almost immaterial. There is a much closer relation between his drawings and cuttings than between Picasso's collages and drawings. The series «The painter and his model» are a clear example of this.

For the cubists, especially for Braque and Picasso, collage represented a sign of a break. For Matisse, collage was the result that has to follow the evolution of this previous work, spontaneous and fluid. The cubists adopted a provocative and productive attitude, but Matisse used collage to give a final touch to his work while demonstrating the brilliance of his mastery. Almost half a century separated the first European collages from those that Matisse exhibited at the Musée des Arts Décoratifs in 1961.

It was in 1954 that the magazine called «Art d'aujourd'hui» organized a retrospective exhibition in Paris of the historical collage. The occasion served to relaunch the technique among the younger gener-

Tivoli cinema; Georges Braque, 1913. Pasted paper. Louise Leiris Gallery, Paris.

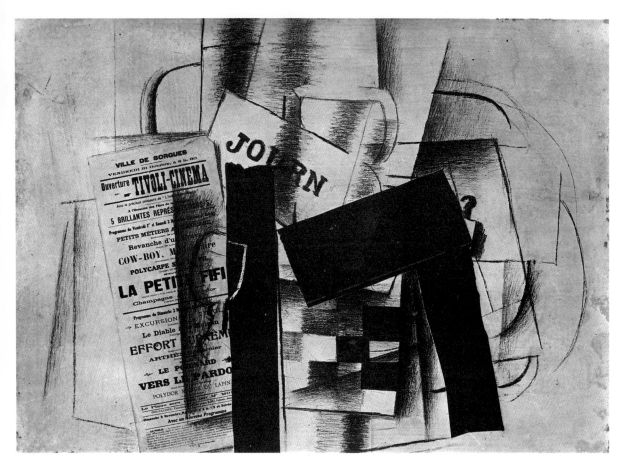

postwar years

The bottle of old dregs; Picasso, Musée National d'Art Moderne, Paris. ©Giraudon.

At one time there was a discussion concerning the originator of collages with painted paper, Picasso or Braque? In 1912, Braque discovered painted papers that imitated wood and marble, elements he liked to use in his pictures. He had the idea of substituting them for painting papers that surprised the spectators while assisting an alternation of values between such papers and the rest of the composition. Meanwhile, Picasso had included a piece of oilcloth in one of his works. The following stage, where both artists worked together side by side (1912-13) produced a series of successes where the chief author is hard to identify. In this work, the concrete element (paint, paper and newspaper) and the abstract element (lines and clippings) each occupy half the composition, confronting each other at one point and letting the spectator apply his particular imagination to the whole set.

Larcave; Alberto Burri
Burri comes after Schwitters, and like him, he used quite simple elements for his works. Old sacking, charred wood, rusty iron sheets, plastics, burnt papers, he used them all to find a freer expression. Here there are no brushstrokes or paint. The structure of the composition is in the thread that unites the different areas of the collage, the folds, the overlapping pieces, the holes. Isn't this theme, at any rate, a reflection of our lives, with its wound and scars?

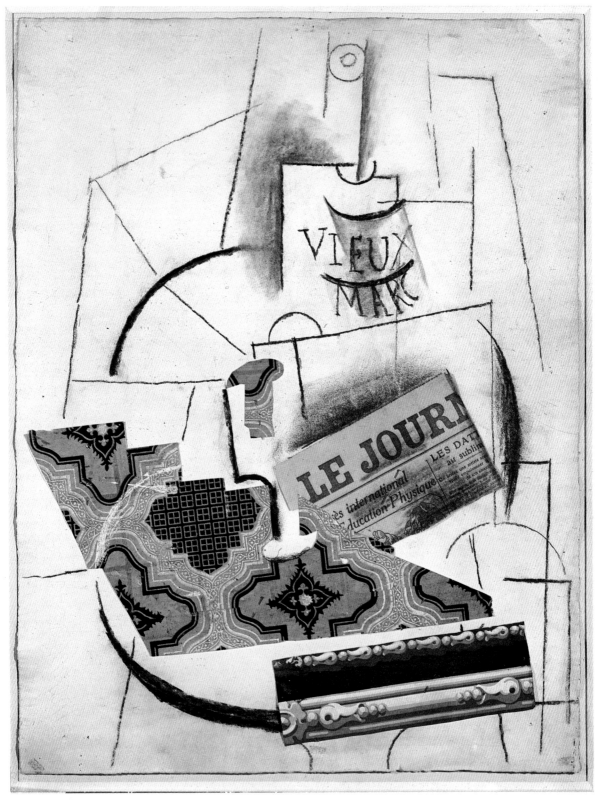

postwar years

Botanic element, landscape with three trees; Dubuffet, 1959. Photo by Robert David.
In this collage, Dubuffet used natural elements to create a landscape, as if willing to demonstrate that nothing is lost, nothing is insignificant in Nature. A leaf becomes a tree and the tree in turn becomes a fossil. Dubuffet prefers the simple art opposed to the cultural tradition that may produce stiffness in the artist. He flees from technique and finds refuge in the ingenuity of the simple.

ations and especially among the foreign artists living in Paris. John Koenig tore up colour papers and then pasted the pieces back; Downing practised stapling; Deyrolle glued fringed fabrics onto cardboard; the Italian Alberto Burri, a follower of Schwitters but with a strong individual personality, used torn sacking, charred wood, rusty iron plates and all those items that people normally reject. Burri's work is surprising, more synthetic than anything seen so far. It takes the importance away from the physical aspect of the materials and places it on the impression that takes

us to the horrors of the war and the physical limitations of the human being. While Max Ernst continued practising the figurative and the surrealist collage alternately, the 1950s saw the appearance of collages done with solid materials by Jean Dubuffet. The artists called them «materiologies». Sometimes, they were made from paintings that had been cut in pieces and later recreated to form rural scenes, or figures. Other times, the artist used materials as diverse as stones, soil and butterfly wings. The Italian Baj created his own world based on the humorous vision of decorated

generals (the medals were real). He used old upholstery, old fabrics, buttons, mirrors... Walls covered by posters partially torn away later inspired the French Hains and Villéglé and the Italian Latella, who presented parts of those walls just as they appeared in the streets. Dufrêne and Aeschbacher preferred discarded wall pieces.
One of the great figurative artists of the moment, Rebeyrolle, also introduced diverse materials in his pictures. Those added elements (soil, iron and steel sheets, stones) act more as a repelling agent to the picture itself than as a

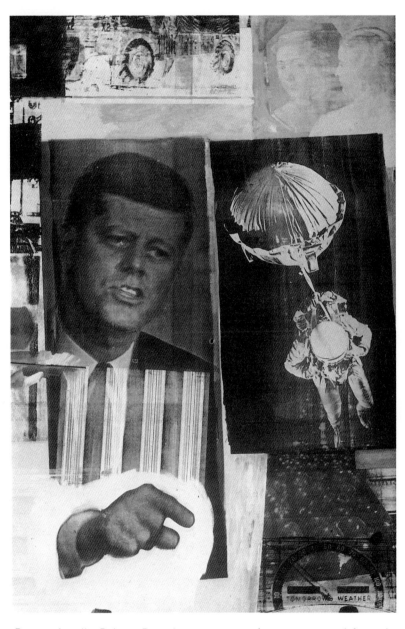

mere search of new ways in this field of art. With Rebeyrolle the dimensions of the picture are too small for the meaning it conveys.

Duchamps had much more influence in the United States, where he retired, than in France. There is, then, an American neo-dadaist school, and Rauschenberg was its head. He also used rubbish and débris, juxtaposing them to the painted part of the picture, where a transferred picture of a current event is often found. The use of elements as dissimilar as a dissected chicken, telephone directories, signs, ties, chairs, umbrellas and so on remind of Prévert's style. When one of such elements did not fit into the picture, Rauschenberg placed it next to it and tied it by means of a chain or a rope. This is the way the artist showed the pictorial cycle: beauty —degraded beauty— rubbish. In opposition to the natural cycle of things, in Rauschenberg's pictures we have the whole cycle.

An American of Swedish descent coming from California showed his compartmented gouaches-collages in Paris in 1964. His work was a nuclear vision of the world.

Retroactive II; Robert Rauschenberg, 1964. Mixed techniques. Rauschenberg was an American artist with high reputation in Europe in the 60s. He was one of the promoters of the combined paintings in which he introduced elements as dissimilar as dissected birds, chairs and food cans. He created images united in a very effective setting and he rapidly became one of the best artists of his generation. For this work he opportunely used some pictures extracted from the «American way of life», with obvious classical touches and a rigorous composition.

6. the meaning of collages

In art, invention often precedes intention. Picasso said: «I do not look for, I just find». The statement has no mystery if we consider the practice of art as the eruption of the subconscious into the light. Braque said he discontinued any picture he foresaw clearly after the first brush stroke. Creation is, most of all, a surprise the artist keeps for himself. To this surprise the artist will add the eventual variations that might appear on the chosen subject. Once this subject has been chosen, the artist enriches it progressively. But an endless repetition of the same subject diminishes its quality. This same principle can be applied to the collage technique.

At first, collage is born as a reaction to the detailed classical painting and even as a way to escape from the aridity of the geometrical abstraction. A collage tries to be a way to approach an object by means of the elements that form the object, whether rudimentary, functional or utilitarian. A collage will accept anything except the purely painted representation, obviously idealized. Instead of a recreation of reality, the collage artist proposes a substitution of a different reality. Instead of the traditional temporal or spatial evasion of the senses towards an artistic work, collage offers us the actuality of current events, of characteristics that belong to our era.

Packing case; Antoni Tàpies, 1969 (170×125×8). Private collection.

Big bed and door; Antoni Tàpies, 1972 (275×330). Private collection.

Artists find in collage a return to companionship motivated by the strength of tradition itself, spontaneous, with common hopes and aims. The social, industrial and scientific evolution played a leading role in that rupture that lasted for more then half a century, even when collage only meant the practice of a series of style exercises. When collage bloomed, however, it was foreseen as an ideal way to return to the essence of a plasticity and spontaneity practically forgotten.

Collage made people change their typical concept of a picture. Collages reconcile intelligence with taste and simplicity with plasticity. It was necessary to find a substitute for the reality around us to be able to go back to that same reality but much more pictorial. That was what collage achieved.

Painting broadened its aims after collage, and the feeling of closed circle was broken. The eyes could see the nature of the world itself, its fragile movement forever frozen in the time and space of a work. Collage later followed two well defined paths. One tended to bring the public nearer through the materiality of a work that occupies a place in space. It is only logical that we refer here to Tàpies, who «excavated» his more representative canvases with a paste made out of marble dust, thus obtaining peculiar effects. He also mixed different types of

31

the meaning of collages

collages made with straw and wood with paintings.

The second option collage offered was taken by some artists who selected its creative impulse, the audacity of its plastic challenge to return to the generic abstraction of the traditional painting, renouncing it for the pure and silent plasticity of collage.

It seems unquestionable that collage helped widen the vision of what was possible in art, a circumstance some abused for commercial profits. Anyway, the artistic career of people like Pollock or Vasarely can only be historically understood viewing their collages. From these to reliefs there is only a semantic step. Vasarely and some others defended the denomination of plasticists against that of painters in the field of collage, which itself could be called the contesting son of painting.

7. assemblies and reliefs

This historical-evolutionist vision of the establishment of collage in the world of art makes it clear that there are three branches springing from this procedure: collage with paper, collage with solid materials and collage with reliefs.

The collage by Louise Nevelson reproduced here illustrates the physical characteristics of a work created by means of reliefs. The collage «Victory» by Saint Cricq, however, is a variation within the field of collages with reliefs. Each element chosen by the artist has its own life and has not been moulded as in Nevelson's collage. We should also mention Arman, whose work was described by some critics as «the piling up of objects within a box.» No doubt all these

works are a completely ironical vision of our times.

Paper, diverse objects, reliefs... materials moulded and used in many different forms by the artists who chose collage as a means of expression. Volume is more important than the flat surface of a picture, but the basic target of the collage artist or the painter is the same: offer the world history, and the public is able to grasp their work, the essence of their truth, of the feelings they wish to transmit, of their creative vision.

Tropical Garden II; Louise Nevelson, 1959. Fonds national d'art contemporain, Paris. ©CNAC, photo by J. Hyde.
Bas-relief formed by outlined boards, metallic fragments and diverse utensils painted a uniform grey. The compartments (some have lids that open and close) offer wide scope for the imagination of the spectator, as if he had found an old trunk in the attic. The plastic expression is wholly contemporaneous, nevertheless. The sculptures by Louise Nevelson are the witnesses of a non-eccentric America, worried about its young, but nevertheless existing, tradition.

assemblies and reliefs

«Victory»; Robert Saint Cricq, 1976, Private collection. This is a small collage (30×44), that appeals to the plastic painter. "Victory" is, in a way, an approach to mythology. Our memories often tell us that the myths of our childhood disappeared behind a thick curtain of outdated phrases and conversative ideas. Myths, however, have existed and will keep on existing in the human mind.

II. THE STUDY OF MATERIALS
AND TECHNIQUES

This part of the book dealing with the technique of collage has been classified in types to help clarify the ideas explained. Our imagination, however, should not be encased by labels that are often useless. After the basic knowledge has been grasped, we will obviously understand that the three types —paper, solid materials, reliefs— complement themselves and match their paths for the sake of creativity. A collage may have some sand if that is what we want. A collage made with painted paper may be a part of another

formed by diverse elements. This group is known as «mixed techniques».

It is convenient to have room to spare for storing material at home or at the studio, wherever we work. It is very frustrating to find the element we need most is missing! We should also prepare a horizontal surface where we can place the elements before using them.

Still-life on the table (Gillette); Georges Braque (1913), Mr. and Mrs. Cl. Laurens collection. © by A.D.A.G.P. Before starting the creation of any kind of collage, I consider it necessary to examine closely this work by Braque. A real masterpiece.
I think the economy of elements used to obtain such an effective result is simply wonderful. The amalgam of a piece of black paper, two pieces of paper imitating wood and a piece of newspaper produces an immediate visual shock. The composition is very analytical and reminds us that Braque was in a cubist period. The collage abounds in mastery and strength and is a definite lesson that places its author in a unique position within the artistic world. Works such as this are a challenge and a guide for our own conquest of the collage.

collages with papers

Creating a collage is like transferring an artist's personality into daylight by means of the papers to be used. I myself have a certain preference for papers that have «lived», that have stood the passage of time. Papers that have been wrinkled or wetted by the rain (see «Sexy» below). I believe they carry a bigger emotional force and establish a more ambiguous relationship with the viewer. But you must look for your own sample papers according to your sensibility and your goals, and these may vary according to your state of mind and many other circumstances.

Sexy; Rotella, 1961. S.P.A.D.E.M.

As a basis for the collage, the newsprint has almost endless properties. It is possible to cover the whole range between black and white, with multiple greys. We can cut it, wrinkle it, wet it or paint it according to our needs. Such paper can accept all our fantasies without ever losing its texture and flexibility (see following page).

saine, équilibrée, sereine ; leur assuré clé en main. La radieuse, tant de fois décrite Le Corbusier, le rêve qu'il succédant à la réalité des encombrées, des sombres , de ce chaos d'ombre, de et de misère qu'avait légué anisation sauvage du siècle, nul livre n'a plus qué à en répandre, à en im- l'idée que la *Charte d'Athè*

temps est-il venu au- ui d'un bilan ? Rien n'est sûr. Aux apologies, à l'en- isme inconditionnel, à l'ac-

lite, n'a que quarante ans. Ce qui en a cinquante, ce sont les réso- lutions élaborées, au cours d'une croisière en Grèce, par les mem- bres du quatrième Congrès inter- national d'architecture moderne (C.I.A.M.), et qui connurent alors une diffusion très restreinte. En 1943, Le Corbusier, cofondateur en 1928 et principal inspirateur des C.I.A.M., les publia, rema- niées, pourvues d'un commen- taire de son cru et d'une préface de Jean Giraudoux, sous ce nom de *Charte d'Athènes*, un titre qui prouvait une fois encore son sens de la formule et son génie

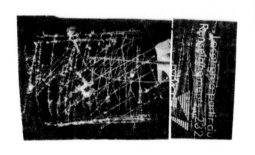

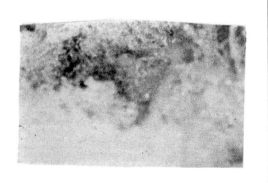

collages with papers

The tools

The basic tools to create a collage with papers are three: a medium-size pair of scissors, a craft knife and a flat metal ruler. They allow our imagination to express itself freely, but for that we also need the materials to work with. Let's review them.

The backings

The backing for a collage with papers should be a thick rigid sheet of cardboard. Bristol board can also be used if the collage will be light. But in case of not knowing how far our work will go, we will be safer working on a thick enough cardboard.

The materials

The basic artistic material consists of pencils and charcoal sticks and, maybe later, gouache or acrylic colours. We will soon discover, however, that the true palette is formed by coloured papers. Two or three resiliant, bristle brushes will help us apply the glue and for more elaborate works, we will need a small sponge and a clean rag. Talking about glue, let me devote a few words to it. The use of glue in collage goes beyond the mere function of sticking papers. Some glues can offend our senses because of their smell or texture. Try them first to find the one that you prefer.
Water-soluble glues are best because of their adhesive power and their convenience.

Working table with materials needed to create a collage.

The glue that painters commonly use comes in sticks or as granules. It is soaked in water for a few hours and then it dissolves easily in a steam bath. The glue keeps its liquid state while it is hot, and it solidifies when it gets cold. If you are willing to undertake these preparations, you will discover the many properties of such glue. It sticks papers perfectly and coats it with a film giving the paper more stiffness. Gum arabic has approximately the same properties but it tends to crack. The acrylic kind, added to water, can be used as glue or varnish. Shops selling artists materials can offer a wide range of clean-working and reliable adhesives of various makes.
A necessary precaution: rinse brushes with water once they have been used. If the adhesive dries on them, you may not be able to dissolve it and the brush is useless.
Let's now refer to paper, the basis of the collage. First of all,

collect a wide range of sample papers to form the «palette», much cheaper than that involved in oil painting, by the way. It is advisable to have three or four folders, 65×50 cm in size, in which to keep and classify the sample papers. The first folder can be assigned to the colour papers bought at the store and white papers of different weights. Canson offers a wide range of colours in all papers they manufacture, while Ingres has lighter tones. These two trademarks together offer a wide range for every need. To our stock add a few sheets of silk paper, smooth or coarse papers, cellulose paper, rice paper, and so on to make it complete.

As you continue making collages, you will be surprised to see how interesting even the most insignificant piece of paper can be.

A second folder can be assigned to newspapers and all kinds of printed matter in general, such as posters, brochures, programmes, newsletters and so on. This kind of paper is fundamental because other layers of papers will be pasted to it. Moreover, printed matter can become an integral part of the finished work. The contents of this folder will change with the addition of further newspapers and as you become more experienced, you will be able to distinguish which paper is coarser, which glossier, which more yellowish...

A third folder should be reserved for the more delicate kinds of paper.

Finally, in the fourth and last folder we will keep the most varied samples, such as pieces of wallpaper, wrapping paper, tickets and so forth. Do not discard anything, since everything has its own characteristics capable of being exploited in a collage.

As an example of this, refer to «Victory» by Schwitters. It shows it is necessary to forget the apparent simplicity or lack of interest of certain kinds of waste paper. When an element is placed out of its normal context it finds new meanings and we discover its true value. The idea, then, is to dedicate this last folder to keep your everyday «findings», such as that piece of paper found in a drawer, or that wrapping paper about to be thrown away.

When an idea for a collage comes into your mind, do not ponder too long about it. Sometimes it is much better to be carried away by a sudden impulse, by the attraction

Filing cabinet to hold the folders in which we can keep the different kinds of paper and cardboard applicable to our collages.

Guitar, newspaper, glass of wine and bottle; Picasso, 1913 (46,5×62,5). Tate Gallery.

collages with papers

(Left): The Sunblind; Juan Gris (1914), Tate Gallery. Juan Gris, distorting the shape, places it in a more concrete context that makes it stand out because of the added relief.

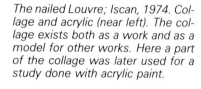

The nailed Louvre; Iscan, 1974. Collage and acrylic (near left). The collage exists both as a work and as a model for other works. Here a part of the collage was later used for a study done with acrylic paint.

«Victory»; Kurt Schwitters (below). In this collage, crowded with fragments of all kinds, we can observe how the most unexpected «finds» can form an homogeneous group. This collage is also significant of the search and later patience of the artist to find, put in order and combine all the elements that form it.

Rough papers have more uses than glossy or satiny papers. The illustration on the following page shows the texture of some kinds of rough papers.

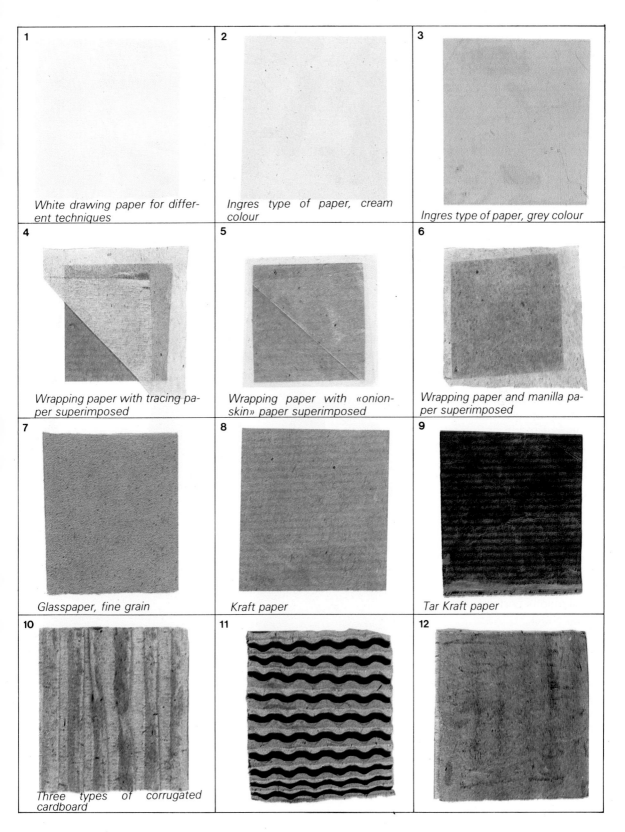

1 White drawing paper for different techniques

2 Ingres type of paper, cream colour

3 Ingres type of paper, grey colour

4 Wrapping paper with tracing paper superimposed

5 Wrapping paper with «onion-skin» paper superimposed

6 Wrapping paper and manilla paper superimposed

7 Glasspaper, fine grain

8 Kraft paper

9 Tar Kraft paper

10 Three types of corrugated cardboard

collages with papers

of a piece of paper, than to plan everything minutely. The sudden idea may appear when you open one of the folders and see the relationship between two different tones of paper.

One more thing: do not try to say everything at once, overdoing your work until it becomes unintelligible. And before getting to work on a definite collage, pay due attention to and review all the different ways to handle paper. It is a material in itself, and the same as a pencil or oil paint, it can be manipulated in many ways.

If we go over the history of collage, we will find out that there are different ways to create a collage, whether telling a story as Max Ernst did (see illustration) or making a figurative or abstract composition as Braque or Schwitters did. In the first example, the material used were pictures or drawings clipped from newspapers, magazines, and so on and placed out of their context. This sometimes produces an unexpectedly funny effect (why not place the image of an astronaut in front of La Gioconda?). These unusual unions certainly create a visual shock.

In the second example, the image pasted on the paper loses its identity. The new plastic form is created, cutting paper with scissors or tearing by hand. Anyway, so you can better understand the process of creating a collage, we will follow it later step by step, considering all the factors I observe while working on one of my plastic compositions. One

final consideration before embarking on the next chapter: a collage has the aim to enliven and create a surface with the elements you like.

Saint conversation; Max Ernst, 1920. Collage (22,5×13,5). Private collection.

The art critic; Raoul Hausman, 1919-20. Photomontage (31,7× 25,4). Tate Gallery.

The Kotsbild; Kurt Schwitters.

collages with papers

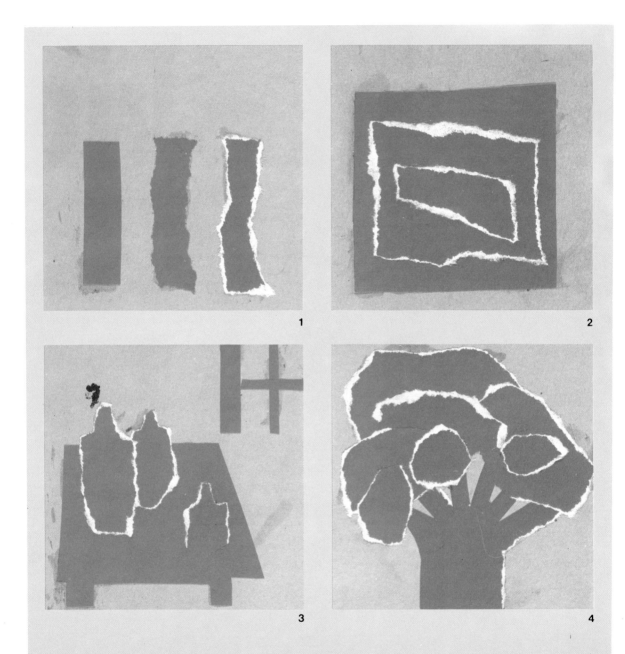

1

2

3

4

A previous study of the possibilities of the materials will enable you to obtain satisfactory results quickly. Here we show the possibilities offered by a sheet of painted paper and the different shapes obtainable.

Three different fragments: cut with scissors (left), torn toward the inside with irregular outlines

(centre), torn toward the outside of the paper leaving a white border. (right)

The superimposition of paper achieves a broken effect.

Bottles on a table: the table and the window are cut out with scissors. The bottles are torn, with the white edge defining the

outline. The bottom of one of the bottles is cut with scissors and thus merges into the table.

A tree: one of the sides is cut with scissors and the other is torn to create the illusion of a light coming from the right. The same procedure is used for the long edges of the branches and leaves.

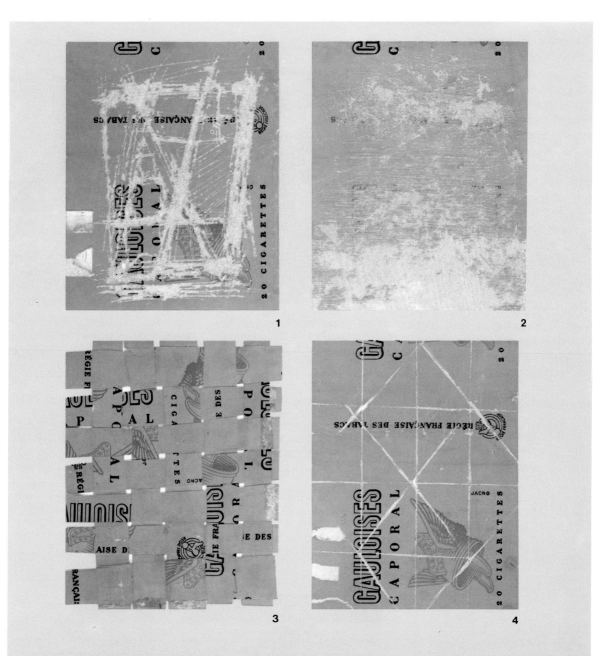

Four variations obtained from a packet of cigarettes:

1. The lines are obtained by scraping the wet paper with a scalpel.

2. Gradation obtained with glasspaper.

3. Strips cut and interlaced. The packet becomes a decorative element.

4. Successive folds and scraped edges produce a geometrical design.

These are just a few examples, but there are endless possibilities. It all depends on your wish to experiment.

collages with solid materials

The creative technique used for this kind of collage is basically the same as that used for collages with pasted papers. In both cases the idea is to put together some elements previously chosen, in a certain order and over a flat space. The difference in the collages with solid materials is that they occupy a space with a very different density, weight and volume from those of paper.

Do you remember when you, as a child, played building houses with wooden blocks? You probably imagined you were the most famous architect when you manipulated those cylinders and prisms. Well then, creating a collage with solid materials is more or less like old times: put together, combine, fix the chosen elements. Etienne Martin, Saint Cricq and Louise Nevelson transformed this practice into something more than a game (see Nevelson's illustration). They needed different tools from those for collages with paper, because uniting solid elements requires quite a lot of imagination and an inventiveness that is constantly tested.

The backings

The variety is bigger than for collages with paper. They must be rigid and capable of supporting weight. Flat backings should be made of plywood or similar, but there are also backings with «volume» all ready to be used, such as boxes, cardboard or wooden

Collage, paper and wood; Louise Nevelson, 1979.
In Nevelson, and especially in this work, the transition between a collage with papers and a collage with solid objects is clearly demonstrated. The general disposition and the use of papers could make it a collage with papers, but the inside of the triangle (top left), with its multiplicity of wooden shapes forming a puzzle, leads us into a very different dimension.

Still-life; Picasso. 1914. Painted wood and collage with fringe and bobbles. Tate Gallery.

containers, frames or stretchers...
Imagination is the main ingredient again, as in any kind of collage. Let's visit markets for old objects and even city dumps, store windows and second-hand shops. The creative spark can occur anywhere.

The materials

Searching for material is always advisable. Success very often depends on the unusual and surprising nature of many elements. Most collage artists, however, consider the following elements indispensable:

—Wood: Fragments from laths or frames; driftwood; pieces of wood of any kind.
—Fabrics: samples of cloth, threads, strings, ropes, old bags, etc. (see illustration by Etienne Martin).
—Metal: barrels, sheets, nails, etc.
Any of these elements can be the basis of the collage but also a complement to other elements. Consider other objects: geometrical shapes (spheres, cubes, triangles, etc.); figurative forms (dolls' heads, lead soldiers, toys). As an example, refer to Joseph Cornel, who used dissected animals, or to Miralda, who adorned famous statues with

plastic toy soldiers. Some artists have employed forks, spoons, food cans... Anything is valid if we can cross the subtle border that separates our fear of public opinion from complete and free creativeness. Saint Cricq crossed that borderline with «The juggler».
Many important collages originated because of a coincidence, a revealing detail or by mere chance. For example, the odd atmosphere of a sculptor's workshop created by the white linen covering the works in progress were the source of inspiration of many artists, who tried to recreate that same atmosphere by

The surprise envelope; Claude Clavel, 1979.
With a very peculiar sense of humour, an outstanding characteristic of his work, Clavel reflects the leftovers of the consumer society. Here some tins become a curious envelope.

collages with solid materials

covering with fabrics all the objects that formed part of their collages.

Since you may not like the final effect of your finished collage, let's see how you can modify it.

Changing the appearance

—Through painting: the collage can be painted over, wholly or partially, thus obtaining a more pleasing finish thanks to colour (see Louise Nevelson's collage on p. 48) Vinyl paints adapt well to all kinds of backings.

—Through fire: collages where wood is an integral part can be broadly treated and modified by charring it. The extent of the burning alters the texture

The juggler; Saint Cricq, 1914 (56×61), on the following page. The fragments put together by Saint Cricq indicate the alchemist's job of the collage artist. A head, a trunk, a doll's leg are necessarily condemned to end up in the dustbin. Saint Cricq ingeniously put them together over a canvas backing and used an old wooden box as a pedestal to obtain this «juggler».

The coat; Etienne Martin, 1962. Different materials.
Musée National d'Art Moderne, Paris.
It looks like just a bunch of pieces of string put together, but if we analyse Martin's work, done with very simple material, we discover a form

to which the sculptor confers a nobility that had been up to then, negligible. One of the characteristic features of a collage with objects is the use of an element or material out of its usual context, which creates a relevant plastic result.

collages with solid materials

and the colour and wood changes from brown to black. The collage is thus coloured by fire, which can also produce a different structure destroying some parts and keeping others.

These last-minute changes only seek to personalize the finished work. The more perceptible the personal touch is, the sooner the collage will reach that dimension that makes it differ from the merely decorative object (in itself an element of undeniable interest, as we can see in «Virgile's dream»).

The Sleep of the Innocent; Iscan, 1977. I linked the papier maché head of a doll to an old picture. The blanket was done with some pasted silk paper and the word «baby» was formed with letters from an old alphabet.

Virgil's dream; Ferit Iscan.

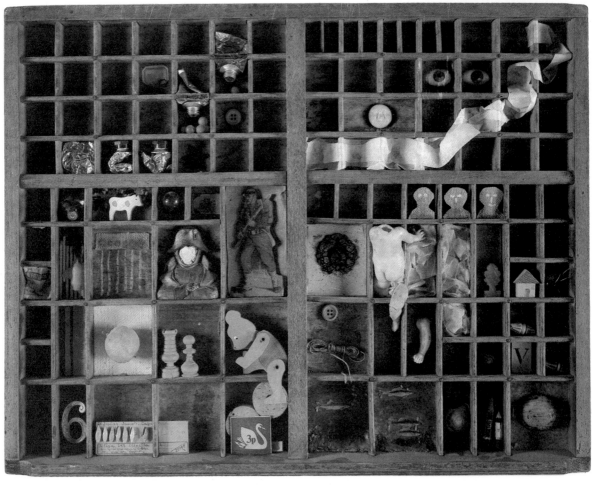

collages with reliefs

I am now going to refer to the third procedure used in the collage technique, that is to say, the collages created with reliefs. This type of work has been very close to painting in many occasions, as with Jean Dubuffet and Tàpies. The reliefs in these artists' collages reach a proportion that places them in a new artistic dimension.

We can say, then, that painting is much more important for collages with reliefs than for the other two kinds we have already seen.

To better illustrate the materials and elements to be used, I have thought of relating the history of «The gagged man» (see illustration on next page), a piece I did by stages in 1979. I used to pile my leftover paint on a board placed in a corner of my working table. Different layers of paint kept piling up until they reached a significant thickness and consistency. I observed that shapeless mound and, remembering Leonardo da Vinci(*) when he advised the contemplation of old walls covered with moss to discover new forms, I thought I recognized the shape of a human head in it.

Le barbe d'Ormuzd; Jean Dubuffet (1959). Oil painting on cardboard pasted over a canvas (77×55), Musée National d'Art Moderne, Paris. Dubuffet undoubtedly has a place among the artists making big contributions to the world of collage. His energy and will to succeed are remarkable. His work demonstrates his wish to combine widely different elements, such as shoe polish, cardboard and sand. His compositions have won him a privileged position in the art of our times.

(*) Les carnets de Léonard da Vinci, Gallimard, 1942.

collages with reliefs

I started working on that board as if it were a game. First, I enlarged the relief belonging to the nose; then, I marked the approximate level of the eyes and a piece of paper was the reference for the shirt collar. I pasted that piece of paper, using a glue. I looked at my «man» on the board again. He seemed to be sad and was quite rigid, and to justify that aspect, I «gagged» him with a few strings nailed directly to the backing board. Now it was finished.

The lessons this work teaches is quite clear: we can wait for inspiration, for that artistic

The gagged man, Iscan (1979). Oil and diverse materials.

The upside down hat, Antoni Tàpies (1967). Painting? Collage with reliefs? The borderline between both procedures is hard to tell in Tàpie's work. Because of the density and variety of materials, we tend to define this work as collage with reliefs.

Fruit bowls; Iscan (1958), painting-relief. Careful planning was necessary before the materialization of the idea. Pieces of old painted fabrics were combined in the search for certain desired chromatic effects.

spark we have mentioned so often in this book, but it is also possible to have an idea and lead our work along the more convenient path. Whatever the case, some technical ideas are necessary.

The backings

Here, as in the collages created with solid objects, a stiff, rigid backing is necessary. The elements used in col-

lages with reliefs are usually heavy, so it is advisable to use wooden boards or thick cardboard as backings.

The materials

Academicism has not yet entered into the field of collage, but even so, it is worthwhile to make a list of basic materials to be considered as indispensable because of their frequent use. Collages with reliefs are of compact nature and their elements are easy to apply.

First of all, we have the colours. They come in the form of powder, not ground in oil as they are in painting. Then comes sand, kept in three different containers, one for each coarseness. And finally, there is sawdust. In the special shops we can also buy crushed plastic, in several qualities and degrees of coarseness, which is useful.

When talking about collages with papers we mentioned four different folders to keep the papers in. Now we should look for a shelf with pots and jars in which to store our «discoveries».

The backing to be used must be treated with synthetic latex before starting to work. Then we shall add the elements forming the first layer of the collage and let it all dry for 24 hours. After that, the surface is ready to accept new elements or reliefs (see illustration of «L'oiseau de combat»). It is also possible to treat the contour of the different elements in the collage by means of a mixture of sand or

The combat bird; Iscan (1958). Mixed technique over a sand backing. I distributed the space to be filled out by means of areas drenched with paint very much thinned with turpentine.

collages with reliefs

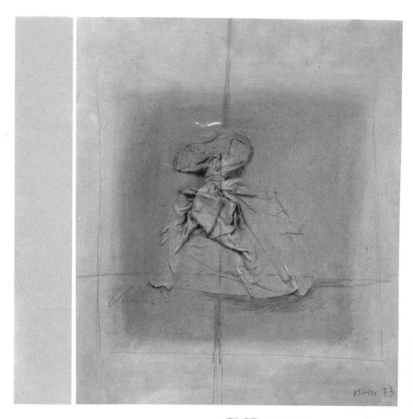

The bag; Iscan (1973), paint and textile elements. The shape and the volume were obtained by the manipulation of a piece of an old shirt. The packing is of pasted fabric and the piece of shirt was pasted with glue. I then applied some paint where I thought it was necessary, until I obtained a result I considered satisfactory.

«D» as in Dorgone; Iscan (1974). Mixed techniques. Paper paste is the general backing for collages with papers, with objects and with reliefs. The letter D, discovered by chance, is the leading motif for this collage.

sawdust with acrylic glue (if we plan to work with water later) or with latex (if we foresee oil paint additions). Papier maché is a flexible material that accepts any kind of treatment. You should learn to make it at home, as the old craftsmen did. It is interesting and not very difficult to do. Here is a recipe you can easily follow.

Get a big pan, fill it with water and add newspaper torn in pieces. Twenty-four hours later start cooking it at low heat and tear the paper some more until it looks mashed. Once the paste attains a consistent texture, add painter's glue (prepared the day before). Now the paper paste is ready and you can add some powdered colour if you plan to dye the backing later. Stir the paste thoroughly and often and remember it will shrink to a third of its original volume when it dries. Use wet paste to model the relief over the backing board. The work will be solid and tough once it dries.

Objects and fragments

A collage with reliefs can take different objects. A word of warning, though: the chosen elements must not exceed a certain thickness, because if the work reaches a three-dimensional stage, it will be considered a sculpture. Taking into account the elements I myself have used sometimes, I can suggest you use cigarette boxes, matches (see «The rainbow»), keys, nails, glasses (see illustration), gloves and most of all, fabrics, due to their ability to be applied flat.

In the storm; Gilbert Pélissier (1978). Devastated by a fire produced by the author, this car stands out as a work that is very close to painting. It is simple and elaborate at the same time. It is also doubly interesting because Pélissier, who is very strict in the construction of his works, has found the necessary creative spark.

collages with reliefs

In the collages with solid elements, these usually keep their original nature, but in the collages with reliefs they require a treatment that unites them to the backing surface. Here is where the sand and sawdust mentioned earlier come in, but only you decide which one is best for your work.

A last piece of advice: do not over-use objects carrying lettering or trademarks (food cans and so on). It is much better to use other elements with more meaning, or more decorative, such as seashells, dry butterflies... Remember you are an artist. Invent new solutions!

The motorist Iscan.

The rainbow; Iscan (1974), mixed techniques.
I have chosen this relief because it illustrates well the difficulty to classify some types of collages. As a matter of fact, painting and collage go together in my work, giving the landscape an unexpected structure. All the elements have been pasted over the plywood backing. The integration takes place progressively, as follows: a cloud escapes from the foreground, left; the cigarette packets suggest hazy clouds. The composition is finished with the help of paint and the impression of a landscape is much more evident. I think this is a good example of the appropriateness of the expression «mixed techniques» on some occasions.

III. THE PRACTICE
OF COLLAGE

collages with papers

In this chapter I will describe the different steps in the creation of a collage, whether with papers, solid materials or with reliefs. I will review all technical difficulties I had to overcome in order to reach the desired result.

1. I have put a group of chosen papers over my working table. While studying them, and knowing that I can alter their placement during the creation process, I decide to use old papers as the basis for my collage.

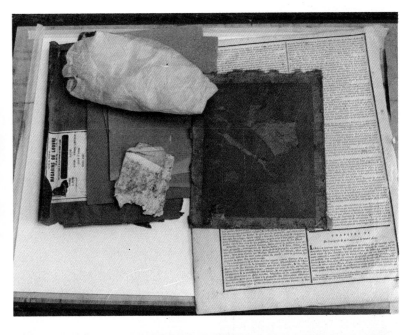

2. I use a piece of plywood as backing and choose a page from an old book as background. I paste the paper, very evenly, with any kind of glue. The brush helps me smooth out the pasted page.

collages with papers

3. I place a few pieces of paper over the background and observe the effect. The image of the Louvre Museum comes to my mind... That worn old blue envelope could make a nice sky... Starting off from that idea, I go on fixing those elements and keep the unused area of the background for something to include later, but without paying much attention to its future shape, size or configuration.

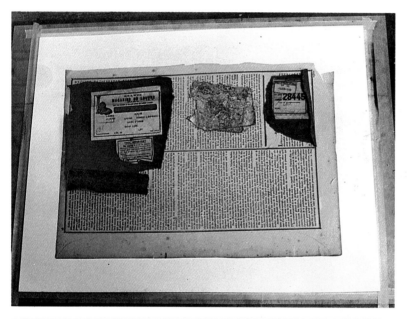

4. I paste the elements that seem to have found their place and build an urban perspective with more pieces of paper. I have very worn old paper in my folder, I will use it to create the effect of old walls. The first step is almost concluded. I only have to choose the papers that will let me build the city now.

5. I create a composition from my particular point of view. I use the scissors to make the profile of the roofs more clearly defined and paste the pieces of paper progressively. I see they get along well together and form a coherent group and knowing that if I am not satisfied I can cover some areas again, I decide to go on. Sometimes it is advisable to keep some of the elements of the collage unchanged, so they can be used as reference for depth and density.

6. Everything I wanted to place is already pasted and the composition is taking shape. It is time to pause, take a few steps away from the collage and think about its finishing touches.
I see a label that has come too evident. I will have to lessen its visual impact by integrating it into the sky while accentuating the perspective, stabilizing and enriching the walls with darker tones... I go back to my folders looking for papers that will serve my purpose.

collages with papers

7. I think the essential has been done. I found some fantastic black in some pieces of tarred Kraft paper, a bituminous material that matches the urban atmosphere of the collage. I have made the sky bigger with a few pieces of blue paper, and with all these changes, the label has lost power and has been relegated to a second plane. We are not very far from the final state.
I refer to my folder containing delicate pieces of paper for those pieces with which I can conclude my collage.

8. A few finishing touches to end my work. I have scraped the sky to make it a lighter blue.

In my opinion, the collage is finished. Deciding whether something is finished or not in art is always a hard and subjective decision to make. For example, why not work on the houses some more right now? Or why not make the landscape much more detailed? We could do it, of course, but an excess of perception would take spontaneity away, and the nature of my collage, in fact of any collage, is based on its spontaneity. No, I stop. The collage —my collage— is a fact.

collages with solid materials

When an artist feels the urge to create, he does not necessarily have a clear idea as to what the finished result may be. In painting there is a conventional scheme that leads to the finished picture. Choose a subject, make a fast sketch, then the drawing comes. It is possible to foresee almost completely the final result, the final image, the shape, the materials to be used and so on.

But in the creation of a collage with solid materials the different elements and objects are tyrants that impose their law most of the time (as we can see in «Small library» by Kristofori). With this idea in mind I will create a collage without following a preconceived notion but somewhat at random.

Small library; Kristofori, 1980, mixed collage. Caroline Corre Gallery, Paris.

collages with solid materials

1. I have a collection of several objects and elements always kept in a trunk in my studio, awaiting for the moment to use them.
For example, here we have a few model plane propellers. Their shape attracted me immediately and the wish to use them made me choose a backing that would keep their function unhindered. A frame would be just right...

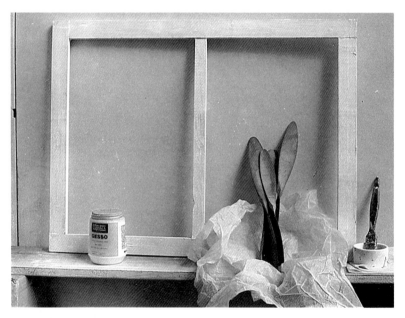

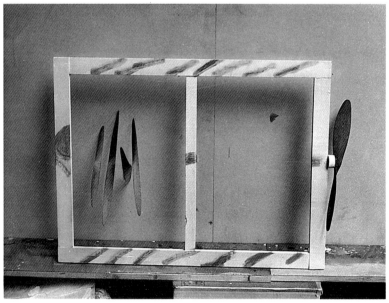

2. The idea of a flying machine becomes consistant in my mind and leads my work. I have painted the frame white and try a first arrangement of the propellers. I make two holes on the sides of the frame to fit the axis where the propellers go. The whole set is very fragile and it is necessary to consolidate it before going on.

3. I have substituted the nylon thread —too thin— by a piece of wire. The propellers are well fixed now. I think I know now where I want to go. The frame will be the skeleton but I must fill it up to justify its aspect. The flying machine seems devised to transport something... Frame, fabric...

The idea of some fabric suddenly appears. I wonder if some painted fabric could be of any use. Let's try...

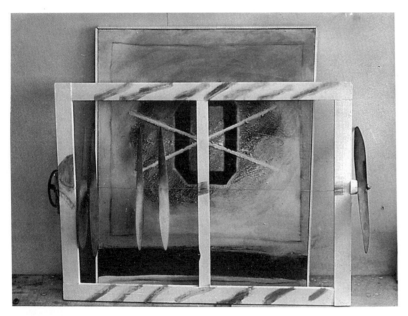

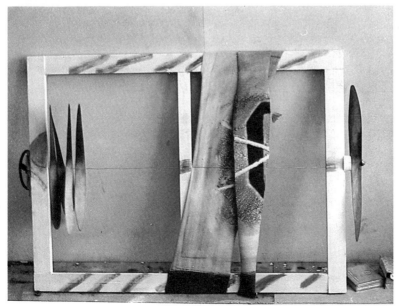

4. All planes have a licence number, right? Watching over the objects kept in my trunk I find a piece of fabric with an «O» painted on it. I tear it and cut it in strips that can suggest the planes in that film(*).

(*) The author refers to the film «Those crazy people in their flying machines», based on the first flying devices that moved through the air.

collages with solid materials

5. After a few more tries, I join the strips together so they can give the idea of movement. I start seeing what the finished work will be like, but it needs more «rhythm».
I have to «tune» the whole set —as I would with a piano— by painting some areas of the collage. It becomes more clearly defined, because the elements I have used (wood, fabric, propellers, wires) offer a concrete and clear idea of an old airplane.

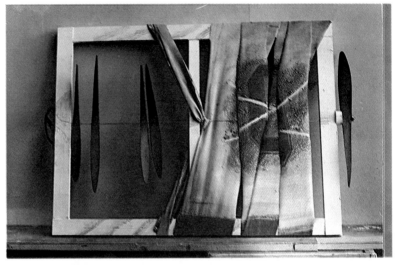

6. I think white makes the frame somewhat «hard», so I paint it again, grey this time. The rear part looks too empty, so I decide to add a sort of wing to complete it. A piece of board cut for the purpose will do.
I am reaching the end, and improvising is now over. I have to study the way to make the composition more rotund.

7. I have painted one of the propellers red and decide to give the frame a few colourful touches. Notice the colour spots do not intend to be pictorially perfect, they are more a game than a technical display. I think the collage is ready now and a name just pops into my mind: «Double O Prototype». I only have to go over the details and add the finishing touches...

8. I noticed there was no balance between the forward part, full of fabric, and the rear part, too light even after the addition of the wooden triangle and the painted zero. I tried an undulated piece of cardboard to suggest feathering at the back, a badge recovered from an old BMW cycle to stress the idea of the plane register number... In the end, I decide to put some fabric over the edge of the triangular board to hide the angle, and there is no need to add anything else.

«Double O Prototype» will not be a combat machine, but a peaceful messenger of dreams and plastic creativeness.

collages with reliefs

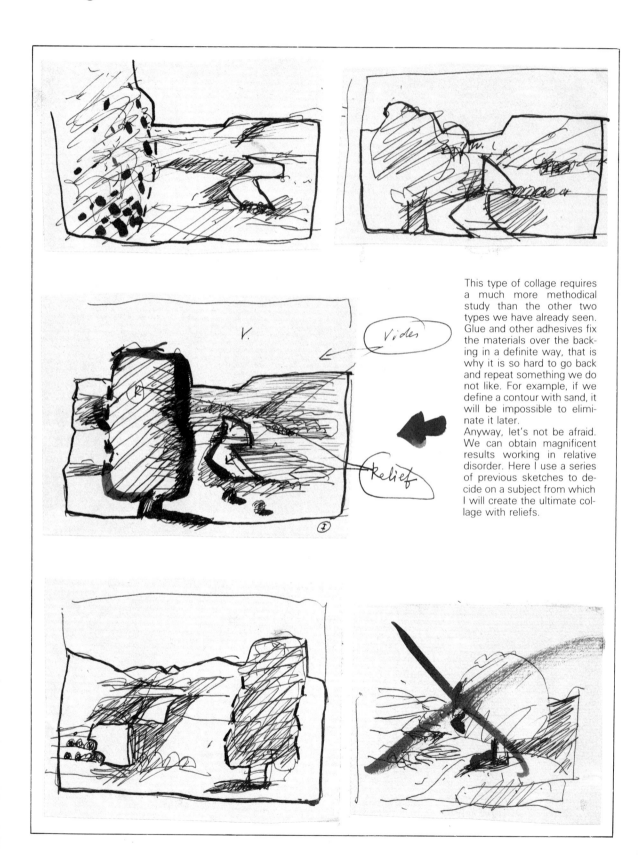

This type of collage requires a much more methodical study than the other two types we have already seen. Glue and other adhesives fix the materials over the backing in a definite way, that is why it is so hard to go back and repeat something we do not like. For example, if we define a contour with sand, it will be impossible to eliminate it later.

Anyway, let's not be afraid. We can obtain magnificent results working in relative disorder. Here I use a series of previous sketches to decide on a subject from which I will create the ultimate collage with reliefs.

1. In front of me, the essential elements I plan to use: a piece of plywood, the same size as the frame (65×54 cm) and headless nails to attach one to the other; acrylic «Gesso» for the background —three successive coats—; powdered colour; fine sand; acrylic gloss medium for pasting. I decide to use acrylic products in this collage, because they dry fast and are easy to work with.

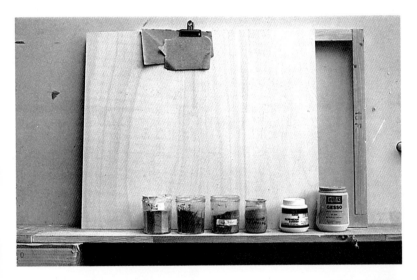

2. Once the backing is ready, I make a simple sketch from the original scheme and accentuate some areas I intend to give relief to: a tree, some hills... I draw the bed of the river but leave it blank to give the idea of depth.

collages with reliefs

3. I fill the areas previously drawn with an even coating of acrylic medium. I sprinkle fine sand over them and let it all dry (about 20 minutes). I use fine sand first because it is always better to start with a finer texture that permits an increase in thickness if necessary. I eliminate the leftover sand and the first image in relief appears. The sky and the river stand out from the group and I make sure the relief of the tree is in the foreground.

4. I draw the shapes again to appraise what has been done. I have to define some elements of the landscape so the landscape itself can stand out. With a mixture of sand and powdered colour I repeat the same technique as before. First I apply the medium over the drawing of the tree and the hills, then the coloured mixture and let it dry. The landscape is becoming defined.

5. I have accentuated some details with charcoal and, little by little, the collage attains a relief configuration. It is at this point that I decide to stress and define some areas that could be considered as finished. I go over the hill and the sand on the ground but I keep the tree in the foreground for the end because I still do not know what will be the best treatment.

6. I have added more sand to some elements of the composition to outline their profile and to cross the river with a bridge. Some lines with charcoal stick help make the tree darker. Notice the interesting effect of charcoal.

7. The tree grows in volume and to make it even bigger, I use ground plastic, thicker than sand, with the addition of powdered charcoal and dark earth powdered colour. To paste all these elements, I apply the medium first, then the material and let it all dry. The tree progressively stands out from the setting, but in my opinion it is still too light and not well defined.

8. Once again I use the charcoal stick to stress some areas of the landscape. I sprinkle some ground charcoal over the tree and keep in mind that the shadowed area will have to indicate the source of light by contrast with the rest of the setting. As I have said

before, it is quite evident that some of these collages are closely related to the techniques used in painting. In the present collage, however, I have only superimposed a certain number of layers of powdered colour and sand, without even a brushstroke.

All the elements are now in their place and have approximately the density I intended to give them. The tree, however, seems to float a little in space. I must find a ground that fits the whole set.

9. A strip of sand at the bottom settles the issue. The shadow drawn with charcoal under the tree fixes it to the ground.
The final touch for the tree is a little pastel light green. The

collages with reliefs

relief catches the powder and produces a rainbow-hued light that makes the general tone of the landscape clearer.

The collage seems finished to me. If you have followed all the process step by step you may argue «I would have finished it some more» or «I think it is a little overdone». I agree completely, but that is the point where the artist has artistic sovereignity, whether he is working on a collage or any other type of creation belonging to the world of art. It is only the author who can say it is finished. In my opinion, it is.

EPILOGUE

It has been a long time as well as a long way since that first idea led to the practice of collage. We must not forget the origin of this technique was in painting and later comes back to it through different ways. The collage then becomes a model for other collages; it uses painting and puts itself to the service of that same painting.

No doubt works such as «My pretty girl» by Picasso, «The Sole Dieppoise Inn» and «The newspaper» by Nicholson were possible thanks to collage. Other artists, on the other hand, create a collage as a starting point for the creation

My pretty girl; Picasso, private collection.

The Sole Dieppoise Inn; Ben Nicholson, 1932. Oil, pencil and plaster. Tate Gallery.

epilogue

of a different type of work. Erro, for example, starts from some concrete images and devises a collage that later transfers to a canvas in the form of painting.

The interest of the collage lies in the fact that it is a young art, a real artistic adventure that we can undertake knowing that, if we try, we will discover new ways, new techniques, styles that nobody has tried before.

«Pan with mussels» by Marcel Broodthaears (see illustration) is on that borderline that makes us ponder over the small participation of the artist in the process of creation. But the mussels have been painted with a polyester resin, the pan has been painted partially... Marcel Duchamp went even futher in this respect,

when he used a simple bottle holder with hardly any additions at all. At any rate, what seems unquestionable is the fact that collages and similar artistic expressions stimulate imagination and are under constant development.

I have chosen «Closed for stock-taking» to end the illustrations for this section because it contains a certain amount of data and facts I have tried to explain in this book. It is not properly a collage, it is not done with papers, or solid materials, or even with reliefs. Take a close look and you will discover examples of the three procedures in its structure. If we had to look for a word to qualify this kind of work, I think it would undoubtedly be creative freedom.

Pan with mussels; Marcel Broodthaers, 1964. Mussel shells partially painted with polyester resin in a painted metal pan. (30,5×28×25). Tate Gallery.

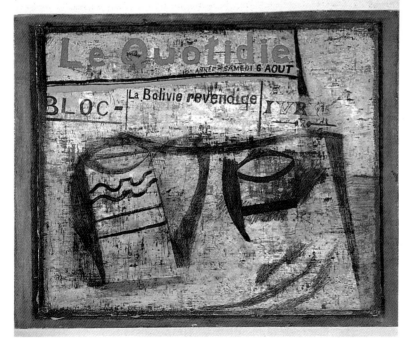

Le Quotidien (the Daily newspaper); Ben Nicholson, 1932. ©Tate Gallery.

Painting-object; Joan Miró (1972) (58×46×20 cm). Miró Foundation. Photo by Zardoya.

epilogue

Closed for stock-taking; Ferit Iscan, Galerie Caroline Corre, Paris.